Cryptocurrency For Beginners

A Comprehensive Guide to Bitcoin, Blockchain
Technology, and the Revolution in the Future of Money
Unraveling the Mysteries of Digital Currencies for New
Investors

TABLE OF CONTENTS

Introduction

The Dawn of Digital Currency

In the last decade, an innovation has emerged with the potential to transform the very fabric of our global financial system. This innovation is cryptocurrency, a form of digital or virtual currency that uses cryptography for security, making it difficult to counterfeit. Unlike traditional currencies issued by governments (fiat currencies), cryptocurrencies operate on a decentralized network of computers, typically leveraging blockchain technology - a distributed ledger enforced by a disparate network of computers. The advent of cryptocurrency heralds a shift towards a more open, transparent, and inclusive financial system, where the power and control of money could move from institutions to the people.

The Origins of Cryptocurrency

The concept of digital currency is not new; it dates back to the 1980s with the development of DigiCash, an electronic cash system. However, the true revolution began with the creation of Bitcoin in 2009 by an individual or group of individuals using the pseudonym Satoshi Nakamoto. Bitcoin was not just the first successful cryptocurrency; it was the first to use blockchain technology to achieve decentralization, a key element distinguishing it from previous attempts at digital currencies.

Bitcoin emerged in the aftermath of the 2008 financial crisis, a time when faith in traditional financial institutions and the systems governing them was waning. Its creation was a direct response to the flaws of the traditional banking system, offering a vision of money that was secure, transparent, and free from central control.

Cryptocurrency's Potential to Reshape Economic Transactions

The implications of cryptocurrency extend far beyond an alternative means of transaction. Its foundational technology, blockchain, has the potential to redefine economic transactions, offering unparalleled security and transparency. The decentralized nature of cryptocurrencies means that they are not subject to government interference or manipulation, appealing in countries with unstable currencies or financial restrictions.

Moreover, cryptocurrencies can make financial services more accessible. According to the World Bank, an estimated 1.7 billion adults worldwide do not have access to a bank account. Cryptocurrency, accessible through a smartphone and internet connection, could offer financial inclusion to millions by enabling transactions, savings, and access to credit without the need for a traditional bank.

The innovation of smart contracts - self-executing contracts with the terms directly written into code - further extends the potential of cryptocurrencies. These can automate complex agreements and transactions, reducing the need for intermediaries and lowering the cost of transactions. This could have profound implications for industries beyond finance, including real estate, supply chain management, and even voting systems.

A New Era

As we stand on the brink of this new era in finance, it's clear that cryptocurrencies offer a compelling alternative to traditional financial systems. Their ability to provide secure, transparent, and decentralized transactions speaks to a growing demand for more open and accessible financial services.

The journey of cryptocurrency is still in its infancy, with Bitcoin and other digital currencies continuously evolving. The road ahead is undoubtedly filled with challenges, including regulatory hurdles, security concerns, and volatile markets. However, the foundational principles of cryptocurrency - security, transparency, and decentralization - offer a glimpse of a future where financial transactions are more democratic, inclusive, and resilient against the central failures that have plagued traditional financial systems.

As we delve deeper into this guide, we will explore the intricacies of cryptocurrencies, their underlying technologies, and how you, as a beginner, can navigate this exciting new world. Welcome to the dawn of digital currency - a revolution that promises to redefine the future of money.

What You Will Learn

Embarking on the journey into the world of cryptocurrency can be as thrilling as it is daunting. The landscape is vast, the technology complex, and the market dynamics often unpredictable. However, the potential for innovation, financial freedom, and participation in a global economic revolution is unparalleled. This guide is designed as a comprehensive roadmap to navigate the intricacies of cryptocurrency, from its foundational concepts to advanced investment strategies. Here's what you can expect to learn:

Foundational Knowledge

- **The Basics of Cryptocurrency:** You will start with a solid foundation, understanding what cryptocurrency is, how it differs from traditional money, and why it's considered a groundbreaking technology.

- **The History and Evolution of Digital Currencies:** A look back at the origins of cryptocurrency will help you appreciate its significance and the problems it aims to solve.

Deep Dive into Key Cryptocurrencies

- **Exploring Bitcoin:** As the first and most famous cryptocurrency, understanding Bitcoin is crucial. You'll learn about its creation, purpose, and how it operates.

- **Ethereum and Altcoins:** Beyond Bitcoin, the world of cryptocurrencies is vast and diverse. Ethereum and other altcoins have introduced innovations that extend the use of blockchain technology far beyond just transactions.

Understanding the Technology Behind Cryptocurrencies

- **Blockchain Technology:** A closer look at the technology that makes cryptocurrencies possible, including how it works, its benefits, and its potential applications beyond finance.

- **Security in Cryptocurrency:** Delving into the security measures that protect your digital assets and the importance of personal responsibility in safeguarding your investments.

Investment Insights

- **Entering the Cryptocurrency Market:** Practical advice on how to start investing in cryptocurrencies, including setting up wallets and navigating exchanges.

- **Investment Strategies:** Strategies to help you make informed decisions, manage risks, and potentially maximize your returns in the volatile world of cryptocurrency.

Risks and Legal Considerations

- **Navigating Risks:** An honest look at the risks involved in cryptocurrency investing and how to mitigate them.

- **Legal and Regulatory Landscape:** Understanding the current regulatory environment and how it affects you as an investor and participant in the cryptocurrency space.

Looking Forward

- **The Future of Money:** Speculation and insights into the future of digital currencies, blockchain technology, and their impact on global finance and society.

Empowering Your Journey

This guide is more than just an introduction to cryptocurrency; it's a companion on your journey into a new financial frontier. By demystifying the complex concepts and highlighting practical steps for participation and investment, it aims to empower you with the knowledge and confidence to explore the cryptocurrency space.

Whether you're intrigued by the technological innovation behind cryptocurrencies, looking for alternative investment opportunities, or simply eager to be part of the financial revolution, this guide is your starting point. Welcome to the exciting world of cryptocurrency - your journey begins here.

Section 1: Understanding Cryptocurrency

Chapter 1: The Basics of Cryptocurrency

At its core, cryptocurrency represents a radical shift from traditional forms of money and finance. This chapter aims to unpack the foundational aspects of what cryptocurrency is, how it operates, and why it has garnered so much attention worldwide. By understanding these basics, you'll be better equipped to navigate the complexities and opportunities of the crypto world.

What Is Cryptocurrency?

Cryptocurrency is a type of digital or virtual currency that uses cryptography for security, making it challenging to counterfeit. Unlike traditional currencies controlled by national governments (fiat currencies), cryptocurrencies operate on a decentralized system using technology called blockchain.

How Does Cryptocurrency Work?

- **Decentralization:** Unlike traditional banking systems, where transactions are controlled by central authorities (like banks or governments), cryptocurrency transactions are verified by a distributed network of computers across the globe. This decentralization is fundamental to its appeal and functionality.

- **Blockchain Technology:** At the heart of most cryptocurrencies is blockchain technology. A blockchain is a distributed ledger or database, shared across a network of computers, where transactions are recorded in blocks and linked together in chronological order. This structure makes the ledger tamper-resistant and secure.

- **Mining and Consensus Mechanisms:** Cryptocurrencies use various consensus mechanisms to verify transactions. Bitcoin, for example, uses a process called mining, where computers solve complex mathematical problems to confirm transactions and add them to the blockchain. In return, miners are rewarded with newly created bitcoins. This process secures the network and introduces new coins in a controlled manner.

Key Features of Cryptocurrency

- **Security:** Cryptocurrencies use cryptographic techniques to secure transactions and control the creation of new units. This makes them inherently secure compared to traditional financial systems.

- **Anonymity:** While transactions are transparent and recorded on the blockchain, the identities of the parties involved are encrypted. Although this provides a level of privacy, it's important to note that anonymity can vary between different cryptocurrencies.

- **Accessibility:** Cryptocurrencies can be accessed by anyone with an internet connection, offering financial services to people without access to traditional banking systems.

- **Global Transactions:** Cryptocurrencies can be sent or received anywhere in the world, and transactions can be faster and cheaper than traditional bank transfers, especially for international payments.

Types of Cryptocurrency

While Bitcoin was the first and remains the most well-known cryptocurrency, thousands of alternatives (altcoins) exist, each with unique features, uses, and technologies. Some of the most prominent include Ethereum, known for its smart contract functionality; Ripple (XRP), designed for fast and inexpensive international payments; and Litecoin, created as a "lighter" version of Bitcoin with faster transactions.

Cryptocurrency Wallets

To use cryptocurrency, you need a wallet - a digital tool that allows you to store, send, and receive cryptocurrencies. Wallets can be software-based (online, desktop, or mobile) or hardware-based for increased security.

Cryptocurrency Exchanges

Exchanges are platforms where you can buy, sell, or trade cryptocurrencies for other digital currency or traditional currency like US dollars or Euro. They play a vital role in the cryptocurrency ecosystem, providing liquidity and enabling users to convert between different forms of assets.

Conclusion

Understanding the basics of cryptocurrency is the first step toward grasifying this innovative and rapidly evolving field. The principles of decentralization, blockchain technology, security, and global accessibility underline the potential of cryptocurrencies to revolutionize the way we think about and use money. As we move forward, these foundations will prepare you to explore the broader implications, opportunities, and challenges within the world of digital currencies.

Chapter 2: The History and Evolution of Digital Currencies

The journey of digital currencies from mere concept to a cornerstone of modern finance is a testament to rapid technological advancement and changing perceptions of money. This chapter delves into the historical milestones, key innovations, and pivotal moments that have shaped the world of digital currencies, setting the stage for the cryptocurrency revolution.

The Precursors to Modern Cryptocurrencies

Before Bitcoin and the plethora of cryptocurrencies we know today, there were several attempts to create digital money. These early efforts laid the groundwork for the decentralized digital currencies we now use.

- **DigiCash (1990s):** Founded by David Chaum, DigiCash was one of the first companies to attempt to create a digital currency using cryptography to ensure privacy. While DigiCash eventually declared bankruptcy, its ideas about privacy and electronic money influenced future cryptocurrencies.

- **B-Money and Bit Gold (late 1990s - early 2000s):** Proposed by Wei Dai and Nick Szabo, respectively, these concepts introduced ideas central to cryptocurrencies today, such as decentralized consensus and the creation of currency through solving computational puzzles. Although neither project was developed, they are considered direct precursors to Bitcoin.

The Birth of Bitcoin

Bitcoin, created by an individual or group under the pseudonym Satoshi Nakamoto, was introduced to the world in a 2008 white paper titled "Bitcoin: A Peer-to-Peer Electronic Cash System." The first Bitcoin software was released in January 2009, along with the mining of the genesis block, which included a reference to a Times article about bank bailouts, hinting at Bitcoin's ideological origins.

Key Innovations and Features

- **Decentralization:** Unlike previous attempts at digital currency, Bitcoin was designed to operate without a central authority, using a distributed ledger (blockchain) to record transactions.

- **Blockchain Technology:** Bitcoin introduced the concept of a blockchain, a public ledger of all transactions that is secure, transparent, and resistant to tampering.

- **Mining:** The process of mining - using computer power to solve complex mathematical problems and validate transactions - was innovative, incentivizing participants to secure the network and process transactions.

The Evolution of the Cryptocurrency Ecosystem

Following Bitcoin's success, numerous other cryptocurrencies were launched, each offering different features, use cases, and improvements over Bitcoin's original design.

- **Ethereum:** Launched in 2015 by Vitalik Buterin and others, Ethereum introduced the concept of smart contracts, self-executing contracts with the terms of the agreement directly written into code, significantly expanding the potential applications of blockchain technology.

- **Initial Coin Offerings (ICOs):** A new way of funding startups emerged, where new cryptocurrencies are sold to investors to raise capital. While ICOs have been criticized for lack of regulation and fraud, they also democratized access to funding.

- **Stablecoins and DeFi:** To combat the volatility of cryptocurrencies, stablecoins were created to peg their value to existing currencies or commodities. Decentralized Finance (DeFi) platforms emerged, using smart contracts on blockchains like Ethereum to recreate traditional financial services without intermediaries.

Regulatory and Societal Response

As cryptocurrencies gained popularity, they attracted attention from regulators, governments, and financial institutions. While some countries have embraced the technology, others have imposed restrictions or outright bans, citing concerns over money laundering, fraud, and financial stability.

Conclusion

The history and evolution of digital currencies reveal a landscape of innovation, challenges, and continual adaptation. From the early concepts of DigiCash and Bit Gold to the advent of Bitcoin and the explosion of altcoins and DeFi platforms, digital currencies have undeniably made their mark on the financial world. As we look to the future, the lessons learned from the past will undoubtedly shape the development of digital currencies, blockchain technology, and the financial systems they seek to revolutionize.

Section 2: The World of Bitcoin

Chapter 3: What Is Bitcoin and How Does It Work?

Bitcoin stands as the inaugural cryptocurrency, introducing the world to the concept of digital money secured by cryptography and powered by a revolutionary technology known as blockchain. This chapter aims to demystify Bitcoin, providing a clear understanding of its workings, its intrinsic value, and its role in the digital currency landscape.

Understanding Bitcoin

At its essence, Bitcoin is a decentralized digital currency that allows users to send or receive money over the internet. Unlike traditional currencies, it operates without a central authority or bank, with transactions and the issuance of bitcoins carried out collectively by the network.

How Bitcoin Works

- **Blockchain Technology:** The backbone of Bitcoin is blockchain technology. A blockchain is a public ledger containing all transaction data from anyone who uses bitcoin. Transactions are added to "blocks" and then linked together on a "chain" of previous cryptocurrency transactions. This technology ensures transparency and security, making it nearly impossible to cheat the system.

- **Transactions:** A Bitcoin transaction involves the transfer of value between wallets. Each wallet has a private key (secret number) corresponding to the wallet's address. The private key is used to sign transactions, providing mathematical proof that they have come from the wallet's owner. The signature also prevents the transaction from being altered by anyone once it has been issued.

- **Mining:** Mining is the process by which new bitcoins are entered into circulation and transaction information is added to the blockchain. It involves using computer power to solve complex mathematical problems that validate transactions. Miners who solve these problems and add a block to the blockchain are rewarded with bitcoins. This reward not only incentivizes mining but also regulates the introduction of new bitcoins into the system, mimicking the extraction of precious metals from the earth.

Key Features of Bitcoin

- **Decentralization:** Bitcoin's most distinguishing feature is its decentralized nature. The network operates on a peer-to-peer basis, with no central authority dictating the rules. This decentralization is seen as a major advantage, offering a level of freedom and independence from traditional financial systems.

- **Limited Supply:** The total supply of bitcoins is capped at 21 million, a feature that is programmed into the network to prevent inflation. This scarcity is part of what gives Bitcoin its value, akin to precious metals like gold.

- **Divisibility:** Each bitcoin is divisible to the 8th decimal place, meaning that the smallest unit of bitcoin, known as a "satoshi," is 0.00000001 bitcoin. This divisibility makes Bitcoin versatile for transactions of any size.

- **Transparency and Security:** The use of blockchain technology ensures that all transactions are transparently recorded and accessible to anyone. Combined with robust cryptographic techniques, this makes Bitcoin highly secure and resistant to fraud.

The Value of Bitcoin

The value of Bitcoin, like any currency, comes from the trust that individuals and markets have in it. It is seen as valuable for several reasons: its ability to operate independently of traditional banking systems, its limited supply mirroring the scarcity value of gold, and its utility as a means of digital transaction. The price of Bitcoin is determined by supply and demand dynamics within the market.

Conclusion

Bitcoin's introduction marked the beginning of a new era in digital currency, showcasing the potential of blockchain technology and decentralized financial systems. Its unique features - decentralization, limited supply, divisibility, and secure transactions - have not only established it as a digital alternative to traditional currencies but have also inspired the creation of thousands of other cryptocurrencies. Understanding Bitcoin is crucial for anyone looking to navigate the world of digital currencies, as it continues to play a pivotal role in the evolution of digital finance.

Chapter 4: Buying, Storing, and Using Bitcoin

As the interest in Bitcoin grows, understanding the practical aspects of acquiring, storing, and utilizing this digital currency becomes essential. This chapter is designed to guide beginners through the processes involved in interacting with Bitcoin, ensuring a secure and efficient experience.

Buying Bitcoin

Choosing a Platform:

- **Cryptocurrency Exchanges:** The most common way to buy Bitcoin is through a cryptocurrency exchange. These platforms allow you to buy, sell, and trade Bitcoin using fiat currencies (like USD, EUR) or other cryptocurrencies. Popular exchanges include Coinbase, Binance, and Kraken.

- **Peer-to-Peer (P2P) Platforms:** These platforms facilitate direct transactions between users. They offer more privacy and flexibility in payment methods but require a higher degree of caution to avoid scams.

- **Bitcoin ATMs:** Similar to traditional ATMs, Bitcoin ATMs allow users to buy Bitcoin with cash. While convenient, they often come with higher transaction fees.

Creating an Account and Verification:

- Sign up with an exchange or platform of your choice.

- Complete the verification process, which may require providing identification and proof of address. This process varies by platform and jurisdiction.

Payment Methods:

- Most exchanges accept bank transfers, credit/debit cards, and sometimes PayPal. Each method has its advantages, limitations, and fees.

Storing Bitcoin

Choosing a Wallet:

- **Software Wallets:** These are apps that store your private keys on your computer or smartphone. They are convenient for small amounts of Bitcoin and regular transactions. Examples include Electrum and BRD.

- **Hardware Wallets:** Physical devices that store your private keys offline. They are considered the most secure option for storing significant amounts of Bitcoin. Popular choices include Ledger Nano S and Trezor.

- **Paper Wallets:** These are physical documents that contain your Bitcoin public address and private key, often in the form of QR codes. While secure from digital threats, they are vulnerable to physical damage and loss.

Setting Up Your Wallet:

- Follow the instructions provided by your wallet of choice to set it up.

- Ensure you create a backup of your wallet, including any recovery phrases or private keys, and store it securely.

Using Bitcoin

Sending and Receiving Bitcoin:

- **To send Bitcoin,** you need the recipient's Bitcoin address. Enter this address in your wallet, specify the amount, and confirm the transaction.

- **To receive Bitcoin,** share your Bitcoin address with the sender. Your wallet will update once the transaction is confirmed on the blockchain.

Understanding Transaction Fees:

- Transactions require a fee, which incentivizes miners to include your transaction in the next block. Fees vary based on network congestion and transaction size.

Making Purchases with Bitcoin:

- More businesses are accepting Bitcoin for goods and services. To pay with Bitcoin, you'll typically scan a QR code at checkout or enter the merchant's address manually.

Security Considerations:

- Always keep your private keys private. If someone obtains your private key, they can access your Bitcoin.

- Be cautious with online services and exchanges. While convenient, they are more vulnerable to hacking.

- Consider using multi-factor authentication and hardware wallets for additional security.

Conclusion

Buying, storing, and using Bitcoin can seem complex at first, but understanding these fundamental processes is crucial for safely navigating the world of cryptocurrencies. By taking appropriate security measures and staying informed about best practices, you can confidently participate in the Bitcoin ecosystem. As Bitcoin continues to gain acceptance, the processes of buying, storing, and using it will likely become more streamlined, further integrating this pioneering digital currency into everyday financial transactions.

Section 3: Exploring Blockchain Technology

Chapter 5: The Fundamentals of Blockchain

Blockchain technology is the bedrock upon which Bitcoin and other cryptocurrencies are built. It's a revolutionary system that ensures security, transparency, and decentralization in digital transactions. This chapter aims to demystify the technology, offering a clear understanding of its workings and why it's considered a significant innovation.

Understanding Blockchain

Definition and Concept:

- **Blockchain** is a distributed database or ledger that is open to anyone and can record transactions between two parties efficiently, verifiably, and permanently. It consists of blocks that contain multiple transactions, and each block is connected to the previous one, forming a chain - hence the term "blockchain."

How Blockchain Works:

- **Creating a Transaction:** When a transaction is made, it is grouped with other transactions awaiting confirmation.

- **Validation:** Transactions are verified by network nodes through consensus mechanisms, such as proof of work or proof of stake, ensuring they are secure and accurate.

- **Forming a Block:** Once a transaction is validated, it's packaged into a block along with other transactions. Each block contains a unique code called a hash, as well as the hash of the previous block, linking the blocks together in a chronological chain.

- **Adding to the Chain:** The new block is then added to the existing blockchain, in a way that is permanent and unalterable. This addition is visible to all participants and can be verified by anyone.

Key Features of Blockchain

Decentralization:

- Unlike traditional databases managed by a central authority, blockchain operates on a peer-to-peer network where each participant has a copy of the entire ledger, eliminating single points of failure and ensuring the system is robust and resilient.

Transparency and Immutability:

- The blockchain ledger is open for anyone to view, making the system highly transparent. Once a transaction is recorded on the blockchain, it cannot be altered or deleted, ensuring the integrity of the transaction history.

Security:

- The use of cryptographic hashing, consensus mechanisms, and the structure of blockchain itself makes it secure against fraud and hacking. Altering any single block would require altering all subsequent blocks, which is computationally impractical on a large, distributed network.

Applications of Blockchain

Beyond Cryptocurrencies:

- While blockchain is most famously associated with cryptocurrencies, its potential applications extend far beyond. It can be used in supply chain management, to ensure the authenticity and traceability of products; in voting systems, to create tamper-proof election results; in digital identities, to provide secure and immutable records; and much more.

Smart Contracts:

- One of the most significant applications of blockchain is smart contracts - self-executing contracts with the terms directly written into code. Smart contracts automatically enforce and execute the terms of an agreement based on predefined rules, reducing the need for intermediaries and making transactions more efficient.

The Future of Blockchain

The implications of blockchain technology are vast and varied. As it continues to evolve, we can expect to see it integrate more deeply into various sectors, revolutionizing how we think about data security, transparency, and transaction efficiency. The potential for blockchain to support a wide range of applications, from financial services to supply chains and beyond, speaks to its versatility and the broad interest in its capacity to provide solutions to longstanding challenges.

Conclusion

Blockchain technology is a foundational element of the digital currency revolution, offering a new way to record and secure transactions. Its principles of decentralization, transparency, security, and immutability not only underpin cryptocurrencies like Bitcoin but also offer promising applications across various industries. As we continue to explore the capabilities and potential of blockchain, it's clear that its impact extends well beyond the financial sector, heralding a new era of digital innovation.

Chapter 6: Blockchain Beyond Bitcoin

While blockchain technology is most commonly associated with Bitcoin and other cryptocurrencies, its applications extend far beyond the realm of digital currencies. This versatility has sparked interest across various sectors, leading to innovative uses that capitalize on the technology's benefits of transparency, security, and decentralization. This exploration into blockchain's applications beyond cryptocurrencies, including smart contracts and decentralized finance (DeFi), highlights the breadth and depth of its potential impact.

Smart Contracts

One of the most significant applications of blockchain is in the creation and execution of smart contracts. Smart contracts are self-executing contracts with the terms of the agreement directly written into lines of code. The code and the agreements contained therein exist across a distributed, decentralized blockchain network. The key benefit of smart contracts is that they eliminate the need for intermediaries, reducing transaction costs and increasing efficiency and transparency.

Smart contracts can be used in a variety of applications, including:

- **Automated Insurance Claims:** Smart contracts can automatically execute claims payouts based on predefined criteria, significantly speeding up the process and reducing the potential for disputes.

- **Supply Chain Management:** They can track the production, shipment, and delivery of products in a supply chain, ensuring transparency and authenticity.

- **Real Estate Transactions:** Facilitating and simplifying the process of buying and selling property by automating various steps, including payments and deed transfers.

Decentralized Finance (DeFi)

Decentralized finance represents a shift from traditional, centralized financial systems to peer-to-peer finance enabled by decentralized technologies built on the Ethereum blockchain. DeFi platforms allow for lending, borrowing, trading, investment, and more, without the need for traditional banks or financial institutions.

Key components of DeFi include:

- **Lending Platforms:** These platforms enable users to lend and borrow cryptocurrencies, often with interest, without going through a bank. The terms are executed via smart contracts.

- **Decentralized Exchanges (DEXs):** Unlike traditional exchanges, DEXs operate without a central authority, facilitating direct peer-to-peer cryptocurrency transactions.

- **Yield Farming and Liquidity Mining:** These are investment strategies in DeFi that allow users to earn interest or fees by providing liquidity to a DeFi protocol, often involving complex strategies and multiple DeFi platforms.

Other Blockchain Applications

Beyond smart contracts and DeFi, blockchain technology is finding applications across various fields, demonstrating its versatility and potential to revolutionize traditional industries:

- **Voting Systems:** Blockchain can create secure and transparent systems for electronic voting, reducing the risk of fraud and ensuring the integrity of the electoral process.

- **Healthcare Records:** Implementing blockchain in healthcare can secure patient data, improve interoperability among systems, and ensure data integrity and access control.

- **Intellectual Property and Copyrights:** Blockchain can provide a transparent and unchangeable registry for intellectual property rights, streamlining the management and protection of digital and creative assets.

Conclusion

The applications of blockchain technology extend well beyond Bitcoin and cryptocurrencies, touching upon various sectors and revolutionizing traditional practices. From smart contracts that streamline transactions to decentralized finance that reimagines financial systems, the potential of blockchain is vast. As the technology matures and adoption widens, we can expect to see further innovation and integration of blockchain across even more industries, heralding a new era of transparency, efficiency, and decentralization.

Section 4: Ethereum and Altcoins

Chapter 7: Understanding Ethereum

Ethereum, often hailed as a revolutionary development in the world of blockchain, extends the technology's application beyond just transactions to a vast array of decentralized applications (dApps) and smart contracts. This chapter provides an introduction to Ethereum, focusing on its unique features, including smart contracts and the Ethereum Virtual Machine (EVM), which set it apart from Bitcoin and underline its significance in the blockchain ecosystem.

Ethereum's Genesis

Launched in 2015 by a team including Vitalik Buterin, Ethereum was conceptualized as a platform that would leverage blockchain technology not just for financial transactions but as a global, decentralized platform for applications. Ethereum introduced the concept of executing programmable transactions, known as smart contracts, expanding the utility of blockchain beyond the scope of a currency.

Smart Contracts

Smart contracts are self-executing contracts with the terms of the agreement directly written into code. They run on the blockchain and automatically execute when predetermined conditions are met, without the need for an intermediary. The introduction of smart contracts on Ethereum's platform has opened up countless possibilities for automating complex agreements in a transparent and secure manner.

Ethereum Virtual Machine (EVM)

At the heart of Ethereum's capability to run smart contracts is the Ethereum Virtual Machine (EVM). The EVM is a powerful, sandboxed virtual stack embedded within each full Ethereum node, capable of executing bytecode. It's the environment in which all Ethereum accounts and smart contracts live. The EVM makes the process of creating blockchain applications easier and more efficient by providing a layer of abstraction between the executing code and the executing machine. This ensures that the code doesn't have direct access to the network, filesystem, or other processes.

Ether (ETH)

While Ethereum refers to the blockchain platform, Ether (ETH) is the native cryptocurrency of the Ethereum network. It's used to compensate participating nodes for computations performed. ETH serves two main purposes: it is traded as a digital currency on various exchanges in the same way as other cryptocurrencies, and it is used within Ethereum to run applications and monetize work.

Decentralized Applications (dApps)

Ethereum's support for smart contracts has enabled the development of decentralized applications (dApps). These applications run on the blockchain and are not controlled by any single entity, offering a new way of interacting with technology and the internet. dApps can range from games and financial services to social networks and decentralized exchanges.

Decentralized Autonomous Organizations (DAOs)

Another innovation made possible by Ethereum is the concept of Decentralized Autonomous Organizations (DAOs). DAOs are essentially organizations that are run by programming code, rather than human managers. They are designed to be autonomous and transparent, with decisions made by consensus of its members, who are often token holders.

Conclusion

Ethereum has significantly broadened the scope and capabilities of blockchain technology, introducing the world to smart contracts, the Ethereum Virtual Machine, and decentralized applications. Its platform offers a robust environment for development, bringing the promise of a more secure, transparent, and efficient way to conduct transactions and build applications. As Ethereum continues to evolve, with upgrades aimed at enhancing scalability, security, and sustainability, its impact on the digital world is expected to grow, paving the way for further innovations in decentralized technology.

Chapter 8: An Overview of Altcoins

While Bitcoin and Ethereum are the most recognized names in the cryptocurrency world, the digital currency landscape is much more diverse. This chapter explores the realm of alternative cryptocurrencies, or "altcoins," highlighting their unique features, use cases, and the innovations they bring to the blockchain ecosystem.

Litecoin (LTC)

Litecoin, created by Charlie Lee in 2011, is often referred to as the silver to Bitcoin's gold. It was designed to be a lighter and faster version of Bitcoin, aiming to make transactions more efficient for everyday use. Litecoin reduces the time it takes to confirm a new block in the blockchain to approximately 2.5 minutes (compared to Bitcoin's 10 minutes), making transactions faster. It also uses a different hashing algorithm, Scrypt, which is intended to be more resistant to the specialized mining hardware that dominates Bitcoin mining.

Ripple (XRP)

Ripple and its token, XRP, were designed with the financial services industry in mind, aiming to facilitate fast and inexpensive international transactions. Unlike Bitcoin and Ethereum, which use decentralized blockchain technology, Ripple operates on a distributed ledger database that achieves consensus through a network of validating servers. This approach allows for transaction processing and settlement in seconds, making it an attractive tool for banks and financial institutions looking to reduce transaction costs and times.

Cardano (ADA)

Cardano is a third-generation cryptocurrency that aims to address the scalability, interoperability, and sustainability issues faced by earlier cryptocurrencies like Bitcoin and Ethereum. It uses a proof-of-stake consensus model called Ouroboros, designed to be more energy-efficient than the proof-of-work model. Cardano also emphasizes a research-driven approach to design and development, seeking to create a more secure and scalable blockchain platform.

Polkadot (DOT)

Polkadot is a unique altcoin that aims to enable different blockchains to transfer messages and value in a trust-free fashion; sharing their unique features while pooling their security. It is designed to solve the problem of interoperability by creating a decentralized web where independent blockchains can exchange information and transactions in a trustless way. Polkadot's relay chain allows for the interconnectivity of varying networks, enabling them to work together under a unified security model.

Chainlink (LINK)

Chainlink is a decentralized oracle network that aims to connect smart contracts with data from the real world. Since blockchains cannot access data outside their network, oracles are needed to function as data feeds in smart contracts. Chainlink oracles allow smart contracts on Ethereum to securely interact with external data sources, APIs, and payment systems, expanding the potential applications for smart contracts.

Monero (XMR)

Monero is focused on privacy and security. It uses advanced cryptography to shield sending and receiving addresses, as well as transacted amounts. Monero transactions are confidential and untraceable, making it a popular choice for those valuing privacy.

Unlike Bitcoin's transparent blockchain, Monero uses stealth addresses and ring signatures to obfuscate the origins, amounts, and destinations of all transactions.

Conclusion

The altcoin market is rich and varied, offering specialized solutions across different sectors and use cases. From Litecoin's improvements on Bitcoin's model to Ripple's targeted approach to financial transactions, and from Cardano's research-led protocol enhancements to Polkadot's interoperability focus, each altcoin brings something unique to the table. As the cryptocurrency space continues to evolve, these altcoins and many others will play crucial roles in shaping the future of blockchain technology and digital finance.

Section 5: Cryptocurrency Investment

Chapter 9: Getting Started with Cryptocurrency Investment

Entering the cryptocurrency market can be both exciting and daunting for new investors. With the market's notorious volatility, potential for high returns, and the burgeoning array of digital assets, knowing where to start is crucial. This chapter offers guidance on how to begin your journey into cryptocurrency investment, covering essential research tips and investment strategies to help you navigate the market with confidence.

Understanding the Market

Before investing a penny, it's vital to understand the cryptocurrency market's nature. Unlike traditional financial markets, crypto operates 24/7, across the globe, and is highly susceptible to market sentiment, often influenced by social media, news, and technological advancements. Familiarize yourself with market trends, the technology behind cryptocurrencies, and the specifics of each coin you're considering.

Research is Key

- **Educate Yourself:** Start with learning the basics of blockchain technology and how different cryptocurrencies operate. Resources include reputable crypto news websites, forums, and educational platforms.

- **Deep Dive into Coins:** Analyze coins that interest you. Understand their use cases, technology, team, and roadmap. A project with a strong use case, solid technology, and an active community may have better long-term potential.

- **Market Analysis:** Keep abreast of market trends and how external factors like regulations or technological advancements might affect your investment.

Investment Strategies

- **Start Small:** Given the volatility of the cryptocurrency market, start with an amount you're willing to lose. As you become more familiar with market dynamics, you can adjust your investment accordingly.

- **Diversify:** Don't put all your funds into one cryptocurrency. Diversifying your portfolio can reduce risk. Consider spreading your investment across different assets, including both established coins like Bitcoin and Ethereum and smaller altcoins with growth potential.

- **Long-term vs. Short-term Investing:** Decide if you're in it for the long haul or looking for short-term gains. Long-term investors often "hodl" their coins, while short-term investors may engage in trading to capitalize on market fluctuations.

- **Risk Management:** Set clear goals and limits. Use stop-loss orders to minimize losses, and don't invest money that you need for immediate expenses.

Security Measures

- **Secure Your Investments:** Use hardware wallets for significant investments and enable two-factor authentication on exchanges. Be wary of phishing scams and only use reputable exchanges and wallets.

- **Stay Informed:** The crypto market evolves rapidly. Stay informed about developments in the projects you've invested in and broader market trends that could affect your investments.

Conclusion

Investing in cryptocurrency offers a unique blend of risks and rewards. By conducting thorough research, employing strategic planning, and practicing diligent security measures, you can navigate the crypto market more effectively. Remember, while the potential for high returns exists, so does the risk of significant losses. Never invest more than you can afford to lose, and consider consulting with a financial advisor to tailor an investment strategy that aligns with your financial goals and risk tolerance.

Chapter 10: Strategies for Successful Cryptocurrency Investing

Investing in cryptocurrencies can be rewarding, but it demands strategic planning, continuous learning, and disciplined risk management. Beyond the basics of buying and holding digital assets, successful cryptocurrency investors often employ a range of advanced strategies to enhance their potential for profit and minimize exposure to risk. This chapter explores key strategies for successful cryptocurrency investing, focusing on portfolio diversification, risk management, and other techniques that can help navigate the volatile crypto market.

Portfolio Diversification

Diversification is a fundamental investment principle that involves spreading your investments across various assets to reduce risk. In the context of cryptocurrency:

- **Across Asset Classes:** Consider diversifying not just within cryptocurrencies but across different asset classes, such as stocks, bonds, and real estate, to hedge against crypto market volatility.

- **Within the Crypto Market:** Diversify your crypto holdings across different types of cryptocurrencies, including large-cap coins like Bitcoin and Ethereum for stability and selected small to mid-cap altcoins for growth potential.

Risk Management

Effective risk management is crucial in the volatile cryptocurrency market. Implementing strategies to protect your investment can help mitigate losses during downturns:

- **Set Stop-Loss Orders:** Use stop-loss orders to automatically sell your assets at a predetermined price, limiting potential losses.

- **Position Sizing:** Allocate only a portion of your portfolio to high-risk investments. A common rule of thumb is not to risk more than 1-2% of your total portfolio on a single trade.

- **Regular Rebalancing:** Periodically adjust your portfolio to maintain your desired asset allocation, ensuring that no single investment disproportionately affects your overall portfolio's risk.

Dollar-Cost Averaging (DCA)

Dollar-cost averaging involves regularly investing a fixed amount of money into an asset, regardless of its price, reducing the impact of volatility on the overall purchase. This strategy can be particularly effective in the crypto market, allowing investors to build their positions gradually without trying to time the market.

Stay Informed and Continue Learning

The cryptocurrency market is rapidly evolving, with new developments, technologies, and regulatory changes that can impact prices:

- **Follow Industry News:** Stay updated with the latest cryptocurrency news, technological advancements, and regulatory developments.

- **Educate Yourself:** Continuously educate yourself about new cryptocurrencies, investment strategies, and market analysis techniques.

Utilize Technical Analysis

Technical analysis involves analyzing historical price action and trading volumes to forecast future price movements. Learning to read charts, identify trends, and understand indicators can provide insights into market sentiment and potential price movements:

- **Chart Patterns:** Familiarize yourself with common chart patterns and what they indicate about market sentiment.

- **Indicators:** Use technical indicators like moving averages, Relative Strength Index (RSI), and MACD to make more informed trading decisions.

Embrace a Long-Term Perspective

While short-term trading can be profitable, it requires considerable time, expertise, and emotional discipline. For many investors, adopting a long-term perspective, focusing on fundamentally strong cryptocurrencies, and holding through market ups and downs can be a more sustainable strategy.

Conclusion

Successful cryptocurrency investing requires a blend of strategic planning, ongoing education, and disciplined risk management. By diversifying your portfolio, managing risk effectively, and staying informed about market developments, you can navigate the complexities of the crypto market. Remember, while these strategies can help mitigate risk, they cannot eliminate it entirely. Always invest with caution and consider your financial situation and risk tolerance before making investment decisions.

Section 6: Security and Risks

Chapter 11: Securing Your Cryptocurrency

In the realm of cryptocurrency, the digital nature of assets makes security paramount. As the value and popularity of cryptocurrencies have soared, so too has the attention of hackers and scammers seeking to exploit vulnerabilities. Protecting your investments requires diligence and an understanding of best practices in cryptocurrency security. This chapter outlines essential measures to safeguard your digital assets from potential threats.

Use Hardware Wallets for Significant Holdings

Hardware wallets, also known as cold wallets, store your private keys offline on a physical device, making them immune to online hacking attempts. For substantial cryptocurrency holdings, hardware wallets offer the highest security level. Popular options include Ledger Nano S and Trezor.

Enable Two-Factor Authentication (2FA)

Two-factor authentication adds an extra layer of security to your online accounts, including cryptocurrency exchanges and wallets. 2FA requires a second form of verification beyond just a password, typically a code sent to your mobile device or generated by an app like Google Authenticator.

Beware of Phishing Scams

Phishing scams are common in the cryptocurrency world, where scammers attempt to trick individuals into revealing sensitive information, such as wallet passwords or private keys, through fake emails or websites. Always double-check URLs, and never click on suspicious links or attachments. Remember, legitimate companies will never ask for your private keys.

Use Secure and Unique Passwords

Create strong, unique passwords for each cryptocurrency-related account, and avoid reusing passwords across different sites. Consider using a password manager to generate and store complex passwords securely.

Keep Software Updated

Ensure that the software on your devices, including wallets, operating systems, and antivirus programs, is always up to date. Software updates often include security patches that protect against new vulnerabilities.

Regularly Backup Your Wallet

Backup your wallet's private keys or recovery phrases and store them in a secure location, such as a safe deposit box. This ensures that you can regain access to your assets even if your device is lost, stolen, or damaged. Remember to encrypt backup files for added security.

Be Cautious with Public Wi-Fi

Public Wi-Fi networks are less secure and can be hotspots for hackers looking to intercept sensitive data. Avoid accessing your cryptocurrency accounts or performing transactions when connected to public Wi-Fi. Use a virtual private network (VPN) for an added layer of security.

Educate Yourself About Crypto Security

Stay informed about the latest security threats and protective measures in the cryptocurrency space. Knowledge is your best defense against scams and hacking attempts.

Conclusion

Securing your cryptocurrency investments requires a proactive approach and adherence to best practices in digital security. By utilizing hardware wallets for significant holdings, enabling two-factor authentication, staying vigilant against phishing scams, and following the additional measures outlined above, you can significantly reduce the risk of losing your digital assets to hackers and scammers. Remember, the responsibility for securing your cryptocurrency rests with you, and taking the necessary steps to protect your investments is essential for any serious investor.

Chapter 12: Understanding the Risks and How to Mitigate Them

Investing in cryptocurrencies can offer substantial rewards, but it also comes with significant risks. The volatility, regulatory uncertainty, and security concerns surrounding digital currencies can pose challenges to investors. Recognizing these risks and learning how to mitigate them is crucial for anyone looking to navigate the cryptocurrency market successfully. This chapter provides a realistic overview of the primary risks involved in cryptocurrency investments and offers strategies to help manage and reduce these risks.

Market Volatility

Cryptocurrencies are renowned for their extreme volatility, with prices capable of significant fluctuations within very short periods. This volatility is driven by factors including market sentiment, news events, and large trades by influential investors.

Mitigation Strategies:

- **Diversification:** Spread your investments across various assets to reduce risk.

- **Long-term Perspective:** Consider holding investments over a longer period to ride out short-term volatility.

- **Set Limits:** Establish clear goals and limits for profits and losses to manage risk effectively.

Regulatory Risks

The regulatory environment for cryptocurrencies remains uncertain and varies significantly by country. Regulatory changes can have profound effects on the market, influencing which coins are available for trading and how cryptocurrencies are taxed.

Mitigation Strategies:

- **Stay Informed:** Keep up to date with regulatory developments in the jurisdictions relevant to your investments.

- **Compliance:** Ensure compliance with all regulatory requirements for reporting and taxes to avoid legal penalties.

- **Geographic Diversification:** Consider geographic diversification to mitigate the impact of regulatory changes in any single region.

Security Risks

The digital nature of cryptocurrencies makes them susceptible to hacking, phishing, and other forms of cyber theft. Investors must be vigilant in securing their assets against these threats.

Mitigation Strategies:

- **Use Hardware Wallets:** Store large amounts of cryptocurrencies in hardware wallets to keep them offline and secure.

- **Enable 2FA:** Use two-factor authentication for additional security on exchanges and wallets.

- **Be Cautious:** Remain vigilant against phishing attempts and only use reputable exchanges and wallets.

Fraud and Scams

The cryptocurrency space, unfortunately, has its share of scams and fraudulent schemes, including Ponzi schemes, fake ICOs, and exit scams.

Mitigation Strategies:

- **Research:** Conduct thorough research before investing in any project, checking for credibility, team background, and community feedback.

- **Beware of Unrealistic Promises:** Be wary of investments that promise guaranteed or unusually high returns.

- **Use Trusted Platforms:** Invest through well-known and reputable platforms to reduce the risk of fraud.

Operational Risks

Operational risks include the risk of loss from inadequate or failed internal processes, people, systems, or external events. This encompasses exchange outages, loss of wallet access, and errors in transactions.

Mitigation Strategies:

- **Backup Your Data:** Regularly backup your wallet's recovery phrases or private keys.

- **Use Reliable Services:** Choose exchanges and wallets with strong track records of reliability and customer service.

- **Double-Check Transactions:** Always double-check addresses and transaction details before sending cryptocurrencies.

Conclusion

While the potential for high returns can make cryptocurrency an attractive investment, it's essential to approach the market with caution and an understanding of the risks involved. By employing strategies such as diversification, staying informed about regulatory changes, prioritizing security, conducting thorough research, and maintaining a disciplined approach to risk management, investors can better protect their assets and navigate the complexities of the cryptocurrency market.

Section 7: Legal and Regulatory Landscape

Chapter 13: Navigating the Legal Framework of Cryptocurrencies

The legal and regulatory environment for cryptocurrencies is complex and varies significantly across different jurisdictions. As governments and regulatory bodies worldwide attempt to understand and regulate digital currencies, investors must navigate a landscape that is constantly evolving. This chapter provides an overview of the current global legal framework for cryptocurrencies, highlighting the diversity of regulatory approaches and the implications for investors.

Global Regulatory Landscape

The regulatory stance on cryptocurrencies ranges from outright bans to full legalization and regulation, with many countries falling somewhere in between. Some jurisdictions have embraced cryptocurrencies, seeing them as an opportunity for economic growth and innovation, while others have imposed strict regulations to address concerns over money laundering, tax evasion, and investor protection.

Key Regulatory Approaches

- **United States:** The U.S. has a complex regulatory environment, with multiple agencies claiming jurisdiction over cryptocurrencies. The Securities and Exchange Commission (SEC) views certain cryptocurrencies as securities, while the Commodity Futures Trading Commission (CFTC) classifies them as commodities. The Internal Revenue Service (IRS) treats cryptocurrencies as property for tax purposes.

- **European Union:** The EU has taken steps towards establishing a common regulatory framework for cryptocurrencies. The Fifth Anti-Money Laundering Directive (5AMLD) includes provisions for cryptocurrency exchanges and wallet providers, requiring them to conduct customer due diligence and report suspicious activity.

- **China:** China has taken a restrictive approach to cryptocurrencies, banning ICOs and domestic cryptocurrency exchanges. However, the country is exploring the development of its own digital currency.

- **Japan:** Japan is one of the more cryptocurrency-friendly countries, recognizing Bitcoin and other digital currencies as legal property under the Payment Services Act. Cryptocurrency exchanges in Japan must register with the Financial Services Agency (FSA) and comply with anti-money laundering (AML) and counter-terrorism financing (CTF) regulations.

- **India:** The regulatory environment in India has been uncertain, with the Reserve Bank of India (RBI) initially banning banks from dealing with cryptocurrencies. However, the Supreme Court of India lifted the ban, allowing for the resumption of cryptocurrency trading, while the government considers specific cryptocurrency legislation.

Implications for Investors

The diverse regulatory landscape presents several implications for cryptocurrency investors:

- **Compliance:** Investors must ensure compliance with the regulatory requirements of their jurisdiction, including tax obligations and reporting requirements.

- **Risk:** Regulatory changes can significantly impact the cryptocurrency market, affecting prices and the legality of certain activities. Staying informed about regulatory developments is crucial.

- **Opportunities:** In jurisdictions with clear and favorable regulations, there may be more opportunities for safe and legal cryptocurrency investments and business ventures.

Conclusion

Navigating the legal framework of cryptocurrencies requires a proactive approach to compliance and a keen awareness of the regulatory environment in relevant jurisdictions. As the legal landscape continues to evolve, staying informed and adaptable will be key for investors looking to capitalize on the opportunities presented by cryptocurrencies while minimizing legal risks. Collaboration with legal experts familiar with cryptocurrency regulations can provide valuable guidance and help investors navigate this complex and rapidly changing field.

Chapter 14: The Impact of Regulations on Cryptocurrency

The relationship between cryptocurrency and regulatory frameworks is pivotal, shaping not only the present landscape of digital assets but also their future trajectory. As governments and regulatory bodies worldwide grapple with the challenges and opportunities presented by cryptocurrencies, the resulting regulations are set to have profound effects on the market. This chapter explores how these regulations could shape the future of cryptocurrency and what that means for investors.

Stabilizing Influence

Regulations aim to bring stability to the notoriously volatile cryptocurrency market by addressing concerns such as fraud, market manipulation, and security breaches. By setting standards for transparency and accountability, regulations could attract more institutional investors to the market, leading to greater liquidity and a reduction in price volatility.

Enhanced Legitimacy

The introduction of clear regulatory frameworks can enhance the legitimacy of cryptocurrencies as a viable asset class. Recognition by regulatory bodies can increase trust among traditional investors and the general public, potentially leading to broader adoption and integration of cryptocurrencies into the financial system.

Innovation and Growth

While overly stringent regulations could stifle innovation, well-crafted policies can encourage growth within the cryptocurrency sector.

Regulations that protect investors without hampering technological advancement could spur the development of new blockchain applications, services, and infrastructure.

Global Standards and Cooperation

The global nature of cryptocurrencies presents a unique challenge to regulators. Efforts towards establishing international standards and cooperation among regulatory bodies could facilitate cross-border transactions and reduce the risk of regulatory arbitrage, where entities relocate operations to jurisdictions with more favorable regulations.

Challenges for Decentralization

One of the core principles of cryptocurrencies is decentralization, which could be at odds with regulatory efforts to impose control and oversight. Finding a balance between preserving the decentralized ethos of cryptocurrencies and ensuring regulatory compliance will be a key challenge for the future.

Implications for Investors

- **Market Access:** Regulations could impact which cryptocurrencies are available for investment, depending on their legal classification and compliance with regulatory standards.

- **Due Diligence:** Investors may need to exercise increased due diligence to ensure their investments comply with regulatory requirements, particularly regarding anti-money laundering (AML) and counter-terrorism financing (CTF) rules.

- **Adaptability:** The regulatory landscape for cryptocurrencies is evolving, and investors must remain adaptable, staying informed of changes that could affect their holdings.

Conclusion

The impact of regulations on the cryptocurrency market is multifaceted, with potential to both stabilize the market and challenge its foundational principles. For investors, navigating this evolving landscape requires vigilance and adaptability, as regulatory developments can significantly influence market dynamics and investment strategies. Ultimately, the goal of regulation should be to protect investors and ensure the integrity of the market while fostering innovation and growth within the cryptocurrency ecosystem. Achieving this balance will be critical to the long-term success and integration of cryptocurrencies into the broader financial system.

Section 8: The Future of Money

Chapter 15: Innovations in Cryptocurrency and Blockchain Technology

The world of cryptocurrency and blockchain technology is in a constant state of evolution, with new innovations continually reshaping the landscape. These advancements promise to enhance functionality, improve security, and expand the use cases of blockchain beyond traditional boundaries. This chapter delves into some of the cutting-edge developments in the field and explores their potential implications for the future.

Layer 2 Scaling Solutions

One of the most significant challenges facing popular blockchain networks like Bitcoin and Ethereum is scalability. Layer 2 scaling solutions, such as Lightning Network for Bitcoin and various scaling solutions for Ethereum (including Plasma, Optimistic Rollups, and zk-Rollups), are designed to increase transaction throughput without compromising decentralization or security. By processing transactions off the main blockchain and then recording them as a single transaction, these solutions can drastically reduce congestion and fees.

Decentralized Finance (DeFi)

DeFi represents a paradigm shift in the financial sector, offering decentralized alternatives to traditional financial services, including lending, borrowing, and trading. Built on Ethereum and other blockchain platforms, DeFi applications aim to democratize finance by eliminating intermediaries and providing open, accessible financial services worldwide. Innovations in DeFi are not only expanding its offerings but also improving security and usability, which could lead to wider adoption.

Non-Fungible Tokens (NFTs)

NFTs have introduced a new way to represent ownership of unique digital items using blockchain technology. While initially popularized by digital art and collectibles, NFTs' potential extends to various sectors, including gaming, entertainment, and intellectual property. NFTs could revolutionize how we think about digital ownership, authenticity, and value.

Blockchain Interoperability

Interoperability between different blockchain networks is a crucial area of innovation, aiming to create a seamless ecosystem where various blockchains can communicate and interact with each other. Projects like Polkadot and Cosmos are developing protocols that enable different blockchains to exchange information and transactions, paving the way for a more integrated and versatile blockchain infrastructure.

Privacy Enhancements

As blockchain technology becomes more pervasive, privacy concerns have come to the forefront. Innovations like zero-knowledge proofs (ZKPs) and privacy-focused cryptocurrencies (such as Monero and Zcash) offer mechanisms to conduct transactions and share information without revealing sensitive data. These advancements could play a critical role in balancing transparency and privacy in blockchain applications.

Quantum-Resistant Cryptography

The potential future threat of quantum computing to blockchain security is prompting research into quantum-resistant cryptographic algorithms. Developing and implementing these algorithms will ensure that blockchain technology remains secure against the vastly increased computing power that quantum computers could bring.

Conclusion

The ongoing innovations in cryptocurrency and blockchain technology are setting the stage for a future that transcends traditional financial systems and digital interactions. Layer 2 scaling solutions, DeFi, NFTs, blockchain interoperability, privacy enhancements, and quantum-resistant cryptography are just the tip of the iceberg. As these technologies continue to mature and evolve, they promise to unlock new possibilities, enhance security and privacy, and redefine the global digital landscape. The future of blockchain is not just about digital currencies but about creating a more decentralized, efficient, and inclusive world.

Chapter 16: Speculations on the Future of Digital Currencies

The landscape of digital currencies is rapidly evolving, with innovations in blockchain technology, increasing institutional adoption, and changing regulatory environments shaping the future of this space. As we look ahead, several expert predictions and speculations highlight potential directions for digital currencies. This chapter explores these forecasts, offering insights into what the future may hold for the world of digital finance.

Widespread Adoption and Integration

One of the most prominent speculations is the continued growth in adoption of digital currencies, both by individuals and institutions. As blockchain technology becomes more mature and user-friendly, and as regulatory clarity improves, we can expect to see more businesses and consumers embracing digital currencies for transactions, investment, and as a hedge against traditional financial systems. This widespread adoption could also see cryptocurrencies becoming integrated into existing financial infrastructure, with banks and payment providers offering cryptocurrency services.

Central Bank Digital Currencies (CBDCs)

The development and implementation of Central Bank Digital Currencies (CBDCs) are expected to be a significant trend in the coming years. Many countries are already exploring or piloting their digital currencies, aiming to improve payment efficiency, enhance financial inclusion, and maintain sovereignty over monetary policy in the digital age. The rise of CBDCs could reshape the global financial system, offering a state-backed, stable alternative to decentralized cryptocurrencies.

Technological Advancements and New Use Cases

The future of digital currencies will likely be marked by continuous technological advancements, leading to new use cases beyond mere transactions or store of value. Innovations such as smart contracts, decentralized finance (DeFi), non-fungible tokens (NFTs), and enhanced privacy features are set to expand the utility of digital currencies into areas like digital identity, supply chain management, and various forms of digital ownership and rights.

Increased Regulation and Standardization

As digital currencies gain prominence, increased regulation and standardization across jurisdictions are anticipated. While this could pose challenges in terms of compliance and operational flexibility, it may also lead to greater stability and legitimacy of digital currencies, attracting more institutional investors into the space. Regulatory efforts will likely focus on consumer protection, anti-money laundering (AML) measures, and ensuring financial stability.

Interoperability and Cross-Chain Technologies

The future might see enhanced interoperability between different blockchain networks, facilitating seamless exchanges of information and value across diverse ecosystems. Cross-chain technologies and protocols could enable a more interconnected and efficient blockchain landscape, allowing for more complex and versatile applications of digital currencies and blockchain technology.

Privacy and Security Enhancements

As digital currencies continue to evolve, so too will the tools and technologies designed to ensure privacy and security for users.

Advances in cryptography, such as zero-knowledge proofs and quantum-resistant algorithms, are expected to play a crucial role in safeguarding transactions and protecting user data against emerging threats, including those posed by quantum computing.

Conclusion

The future of digital currencies holds great promise, with the potential for profound changes in how we transact, invest, and interact with the digital world. While the path forward may include challenges, particularly in terms of regulation and security, the ongoing innovations and growing adoption of digital currencies suggest a vibrant and dynamic future for the field. As we speculate on what's to come, it's clear that digital currencies are set to play a significant role in shaping the future of finance, offering opportunities for greater efficiency, inclusivity, and innovation in the global economy.

Conclusion

The Journey Ahead

As we conclude our exploration of the dynamic world of cryptocurrencies, it's clear that we stand at the threshold of a new financial era. The journey into cryptocurrency is not merely about participating in a novel form of investment; it's about engaging with the future of money itself. This concluding chapter serves as both encouragement and a call to action for those ready to embrace the transformative potential of digital currencies.

Embrace the Opportunities

The realm of cryptocurrency offers a wealth of opportunities, from the potential for significant financial returns to the chance to be part of pioneering technological advancements. As you embark on or continue your journey, remember that the landscape of digital currencies is one of constant evolution. Embracing the opportunities that come with change, while remaining mindful of the inherent risks, can lead to rewarding experiences both personally and financially.

Commit to Continuous Learning

The rapid pace of change in the cryptocurrency world demands continuous learning. Staying informed about the latest developments, understanding new technologies, and keeping abreast of regulatory changes are crucial for navigating this space successfully. Engage with communities, attend conferences, and follow thought leaders in the field to enrich your knowledge and understanding.

Explore with Curiosity

Approach the world of cryptocurrencies with curiosity. Beyond the headlines and hype, there are profound ideas and innovations waiting to be discovered. From the underlying blockchain technology to the myriad applications that extend beyond finance, the potential for discovery is boundless. Let your curiosity guide you through the complexities and wonders of the digital currency landscape.

Contribute to the Community

The cryptocurrency community is diverse, spanning across the globe and encompassing a wide range of skills, backgrounds, and perspectives. Contributing to this community, whether through participation in forums, development projects, or educational initiatives, can be incredibly rewarding. Sharing your insights, asking questions, and supporting others are ways to enrich the community and yourself.

Prepare for the Future

As digital currencies continue to gain acceptance and integrate into mainstream financial systems, preparing for a future where they play a significant role is wise. Consider how cryptocurrencies might impact your personal and professional life, and begin to adapt to the possibilities that lie ahead.

The journey into the world of cryptocurrencies is an adventure into the unknown, filled with challenges, opportunities, and the potential for significant rewards. As you move forward, remember that the journey is as much about the learning and experiences gained along the way as it is about the destination. By embracing the dynamic world of cryptocurrencies, committing to continuous learning, and exploring with curiosity, you can navigate the future of finance with confidence and insight. Welcome to the journey ahead – a journey of discovery, innovation, and endless possibilities.

How to Continue Your Education in Cryptocurrency

As the cryptocurrency landscape is continually evolving, staying informed and educated is crucial for anyone involved in this space. The journey into the world of digital currencies is one of lifelong learning, where the rapid pace of innovation and change requires an ongoing commitment to education. This final section offers resources and advice for keeping abreast of the latest developments and deepening your understanding of cryptocurrency.

Online Platforms and Educational Resources

- **Cryptocurrency News Websites:** Regularly visit reputable cryptocurrency news platforms such as CoinDesk, Cointelegraph, and The Block for the latest updates, analyses, and insights.

- **Online Courses and Webinars:** Platforms like Coursera, Udemy, and Khan Academy offer a range of courses covering the basics of cryptocurrencies, blockchain technology, and advanced trading strategies. Many industry organizations and platforms also host webinars and online workshops.

- **Podcasts and YouTube Channels:** There are numerous high-quality podcasts and YouTube channels dedicated to cryptocurrency discussions, interviews with industry experts, and tutorials that can enhance your understanding and provide valuable insights.

Community Engagement and Networking

- **Forums and Social Media:** Join cryptocurrency forums such as BitcoinTalk, Reddit's cryptocurrency communities, and social media groups. Engaging in discussions and sharing insights with others can provide diverse perspectives and real-time information.

- **Conferences and Meetups:** Attend cryptocurrency and blockchain conferences, seminars, and local meetups. These events offer opportunities to learn from experts, discover new trends, and network with other enthusiasts and professionals.

Reading and Research

- **Whitepapers and Academic Papers:** Reading the original Bitcoin whitepaper by Satoshi Nakamoto is a good starting point. Many projects publish whitepapers detailing their technology, objectives, and economics. Academic journals and papers can also provide in-depth analyses and research findings.

- **Books:** There are several informative books on cryptocurrencies and blockchain technology, ranging from beginner guides to in-depth analyses of the technical and economic aspects. Titles like "Digital Gold" by Nathaniel Popper and "The Age of Cryptocurrency" by Paul Vigna and Michael J. Casey are excellent resources.

Practical Experience

- **Experiment with Small Transactions:** Hands-on experience is invaluable. Consider setting up a cryptocurrency wallet, conducting small transactions, or participating in staking or mining if you're technically inclined. This practical experience can deepen your understanding of how different cryptocurrencies and blockchain technologies work.

- **Explore Development Tools:** If you're interested in the technical side, explore blockchain development platforms and tools. Many blockchain projects are open-source, offering a wealth of resources for aspiring developers.

Staying Safe and Ethical

- **Security Best Practices:** As you delve deeper into cryptocurrency, prioritize learning about security best practices to protect your investments and personal information.

- **Ethical Considerations:** Stay informed about the ethical implications of cryptocurrency technologies and investments, including environmental concerns and the social impact of digital currencies and blockchain applications.

Continuing your education in cryptocurrency is a dynamic and ongoing process that requires curiosity, critical thinking, and an openness to learning. By leveraging a variety of resources, engaging with the community, and gaining practical experience, you can stay at the forefront of this rapidly evolving field. Whether you're a novice enthusiast or aspiring to be a blockchain developer, the journey of learning in the world of digital currencies is boundless and filled with opportunities for growth and discovery.

Bonus Material

Glossary of Key Terms

The world of cryptocurrency is filled with specialized terms and concepts. Understanding these terms is essential for navigating the cryptocurrency landscape effectively. Below is a glossary of key cryptocurrency terms to aid your understanding:

- **Altcoin:** Any cryptocurrency other than Bitcoin. Altcoins can vary greatly in their purposes and structures.

- **Blockchain:** A decentralized, digital ledger that records transactions across many computers in a way that prevents alterations once a block is recorded.

- **Bitcoin:** The first and most well-known cryptocurrency, invented by an anonymous person or group of people using the pseudonym Satoshi Nakamoto in 2008.

- **Cold Wallet (Cold Storage):** A method of storing cryptocurrencies offline to protect them from hacking. This can be hardware wallets or paper wallets.

- **Cryptocurrency:** A digital or virtual currency that uses cryptography for security and operates independently of a central bank.

- **DeFi (Decentralized Finance):** Financial services, including lending, borrowing, and trading, built on blockchain technology that operate without central financial intermediaries.

- **Distributed Ledger:** A ledger of transactions maintained across multiple locations or among multiple participants, rather than being centralized.

- **Ethereum:** A decentralized platform that enables the creation of smart contracts and decentralized applications (dApps), powered by its associated cryptocurrency, Ether (ETH).

- **Exchange:** A platform where buyers and sellers trade cryptocurrencies using different fiat currencies or other digital assets.

- **Fiat Currency:** Government-issued currency that is not backed by a physical commodity but by the trust in the issuing government.

- **Gas:** A fee paid to execute transactions and smart contracts on the Ethereum network, measured in units of "gwei."

- **Halving:** An event in some cryptocurrencies (most notably Bitcoin) that reduces the reward for mining new blocks by half, occurring at regular intervals to control the supply of coins.

- **ICO (Initial Coin Offering):** A fundraising method in which new projects sell their underlying crypto tokens in exchange for Bitcoin, Ethereum, or other cryptocurrencies.

- **Mining:** The process by which transactions are verified and added to a blockchain, also the means through which new bitcoins or some altcoins are created.

- **NFT (Non-Fungible Token):** A unique digital identifier that cannot be copied, substituted, or subdivided, used to certify authenticity and ownership of a digital asset.

- **Private Key:** A secure code that enables a user to access and manage their cryptocurrency. It is essential to keep this private and secure.

- **Public Key:** A cryptographic code that allows a user to receive cryptocurrencies into their account.

- **Smart Contract:** A self-executing contract with the terms of the agreement directly written into lines of code, stored and executed on a blockchain.

- **Wallet:** A digital tool that allows users to store, send, and receive cryptocurrencies. Wallets can be software-based (online, desktop, or mobile) or hardware-based.

This glossary covers some of the foundational terms you'll encounter in the world of cryptocurrency. As you delve deeper into this fascinating field, you'll likely encounter more specialized terms and concepts, each adding to the richness and complexity of the cryptocurrency ecosystem.

Recommended Resources for Further Reading

Diving deeper into the world of cryptocurrency and blockchain requires access to reliable and comprehensive resources. Whether you're a beginner looking to build foundational knowledge or an experienced enthusiast seeking to expand your understanding, the following curated list of books, websites, and online courses offers valuable insights and information to guide your journey.

Books

- **"Digital Gold: Bitcoin and the Inside Story of the Misfits and Millionaires Trying to Reinvent Money" by Nathaniel Popper:** An engaging narrative that explores the history of Bitcoin and the stories of those who have played a part in its development.

- **"The Age of Cryptocurrency: How Bitcoin and Digital Money Are Challenging the Global Economic Order" by Paul Vigna and Michael J. Casey:** This book provides an insightful exploration of how cryptocurrency is impacting the global financial system.

- **"Mastering Bitcoin: Unlocking Digital Cryptocurrencies" by Andreas M. Antonopoulos:** An essential read for those looking to understand the technical aspects of Bitcoin and how it works under the hood.

- **"Blockchain Basics: A Non-Technical Introduction in 25 Steps" by Daniel Drescher:** A clear and accessible introduction to the principles of blockchain technology, presented in a simple, easy-to-understand format.

Websites

- **CoinDesk and Cointelegraph:** Leading news websites that offer the latest updates, analyses, and insights on cryptocurrency and blockchain technology.

- **CoinMarketCap and CoinGecko:** These platforms provide up-to-date information on cryptocurrency prices, market caps, volumes, and other relevant data.

- **Reddit Cryptocurrency Communities:** Subreddits like r/Bitcoin, r/ethereum, and r/CryptoCurrency are valuable forums for discussion, questions, and community insights.

Online Courses

- **"Bitcoin and Cryptocurrency Technologies" offered by Princeton University on Coursera:** A comprehensive course that covers the technical aspects of cryptocurrencies, how they operate, and their potential for societal impact.

- **"Blockchain Fundamentals" offered by Berkeley University of California on edX:** This course provides a foundational understanding of blockchain technology, including its development, mechanisms, and implications.

- **"Cryptocurrency and Blockchain: An Introduction to Digital Currencies" offered by the University of Pennsylvania on Coursera:** Ideal for beginners, this course delves into the basics of cryptocurrencies and blockchain, discussing their role in the financial sector.

Podcasts and YouTube Channels

- **"Unchained" Podcast by Laura Shin:** Features interviews with key figures in the cryptocurrency world, offering insights into the latest trends and developments.

- **Andreas M. Antonopoulos' YouTube Channel:** Offers educational videos on various aspects of Bitcoin and blockchain technology, presented by a renowned expert in the field.

- **"The Cryptoverse" by Chris Coney on YouTube:** Provides news, reviews, and tutorials on cryptocurrency and blockchain technology, catering to both beginners and advanced users.

The resources listed above are just a starting point for your educational journey in the cryptocurrency and blockchain space. As this field is rapidly evolving, staying curious, open to learning, and actively seeking out the latest information will be key to deepening your understanding and keeping pace with new developments.

Frequently Asked Questions

Entering the world of cryptocurrency can be overwhelming due to its complexity and the vast amount of information available. Here are answers to some common questions that newcomers often have about cryptocurrency, designed to clarify basic concepts and provide guidance.

1. What is cryptocurrency? Cryptocurrency is a type of digital or virtual currency that uses cryptography for security. It operates on decentralized networks based on blockchain technology—a distributed ledger enforced by a disparate network of computers. Cryptocurrencies are characterized by their absence of central authority, making them theoretically immune to government interference or manipulation.

2. How does blockchain technology work? Blockchain technology is a decentralized system that records all transactions across a network of computers. It consists of blocks of data that are securely linked together to form a chain. Each block contains a number of transactions that are verified by network participants, called miners or validators, depending on the consensus mechanism used. Once a block is added to the chain, the information is permanent and unalterable, ensuring transparency and security.

3. How do I buy cryptocurrency? You can buy cryptocurrencies through cryptocurrency exchanges, which are platforms that match buyers with sellers. To start, you'll need to create an account, verify your identity (as required by the platform), and deposit fiat currency or another cryptocurrency. Once your account is funded, you can purchase cryptocurrencies of your choice based on the exchange's available offerings.

4. What is a wallet, and why do I need one? A cryptocurrency wallet is a digital tool that allows you to store, send, and receive cryptocurrencies. Wallets keep your private keys—the passwords that grant you access to your cryptocurrencies—safe and accessible. Wallets can be software-based (online, desktop, or mobile) or hardware-based for increased security. You need a wallet to manage your cryptocurrency holdings securely.

5. Are cryptocurrencies legal? The legality of cryptocurrency varies from country to country. While many countries have embraced cryptocurrencies, setting clear regulations for their use and taxation, others have imposed restrictions or outright bans. It's essential to understand the legal framework for cryptocurrency in your jurisdiction before engaging in any cryptocurrency transactions or investments.

6. How are cryptocurrencies taxed? Tax treatment of cryptocurrencies also varies by country. In many jurisdictions, cryptocurrencies are treated as property, and transactions are subject to capital gains tax. This includes selling cryptocurrencies for fiat, trading one cryptocurrency for another, and using cryptocurrencies to purchase goods and services. Keeping detailed records of your transactions is crucial for accurate tax reporting.

7. Can I mine cryptocurrency? Yes, but the feasibility of mining depends on the cryptocurrency and the competition. Mining involves using computer hardware to solve complex mathematical problems that validate transactions on the blockchain. Successful miners are rewarded with newly created coins and transaction fees. However, mining popular cryptocurrencies like Bitcoin requires significant computational power and electricity, making it less accessible for individuals.

8. Is investing in cryptocurrency safe? Investing in cryptocurrency carries risks, including high volatility, regulatory changes, and security vulnerabilities. However, taking steps such as conducting thorough research, practicing safe storage, and employing risk management strategies can help mitigate these risks. Like any investment, it's important to only invest what you can afford to lose and diversify your portfolio.

These FAQs provide a starting point for understanding the complex world of cryptocurrency. As you dive deeper into this space, continue to seek out reliable information, engage with the community, and approach investments with caution and due diligence.

Made in United States
North Haven, CT
07 December 2024

61952022R00046